WHAT DO YOU KNOW

SMOKING

PETE SANDERS and STEVE MYERS

W

FRANKLIN WATTS
LONDON • SYDNEY

This edition published in 2000
© Aladdin Books Ltd 1994
All rights reserved

Designed and produced by
Aladdin Books Ltd
28 Percy Street
London W1P 0LD

First published in Great Britain in
1994 by Franklin Watts
96 Leonard Street
London EC2A 4XD

ISBN: 0 7496 1552 4 (hardback)
ISBN: 0 7496 3739 0 (paperback)

A catalogue record for this book is
available from the British Library.

Printed in Belgium

The publishers wish to thank all
the children and adults who posed
for the photographs in this book.

Design   David West
                    Children's
                    Book Design
Editor   Jen Green
Picture research   Brooks-
                    Krikler
Illustrator   Mike Lacy

Pete Sanders is Senior Lecturer in
health education at the University
of North London. He was a head
teacher for ten years and has
written many books on social
issues for children.

Steve Myers is a freelance writer
who has co-written other titles in
this series and worked on several
educational projects for children.

The consultant, Amanda
Sandford, works for ASH (Action
on Smoking and Health).

CONTENTS

HOW TO USE THIS BOOK 2

INTRODUCTION...3

WHY DO PEOPLE SMOKE? 4

STARTING TO SMOKE 7

WHAT EFFECTS DOES SMOKING HAVE
ON YOUR HEALTH? 11

WHAT OTHER PROBLEMS DOES
SMOKING CAUSE? 14

PASSIVE SMOKING 18

THE SMOKING INDUSTRY 21

STOPPING SMOKING 24

WHAT CAN BE DONE ABOUT SMOKING? 27

WHAT CAN WE DO? 30

INDEX..32

HOW TO USE THIS BOOK
The books in this series are intended to help young people to understand more about the issues that may affect their lives.

At the end of the book there is a section called "What Can We Do?" This presents suggestions and ideas, helping the reader to develop a sense of citizenship. Organisations and helplines are also listed, to provide additional sources of information and support.

Each book can be read by a child alone, or together with a parent, carer, teacher or helper. Issues raised in the storyline are further discussed in the accompanying text, so that there is an opportunity to talk through ideas as they come up.

INTRODUCTION

WHEN CHRISTOPHER COLUMBUS RETURNED FROM HIS DISCOVERY OF THE NEW WORLD, HE BROUGHT NEWS OF THE STRANGE CUSTOM OF SMOKING ROLLED TOBACCO LEAVES. TOBACCO HAS NOW BEEN SMOKED IN EUROPE IN ONE FORM OR ANOTHER FOR HUNDREDS OF YEARS.

It was not until this century that cigarettes became fashionable. However, people's attitudes to smoking have changed a lot over the last few years.

Today smoking raises many issues for adults and young people. You might be determined never to smoke, or you might be trying to decide whether to begin. Whatever the case, this book will help you to understand more about the reasons why people smoke, and the effects smoking has on health. Each chapter focuses on a different aspect of the subject, illustrated by an episode in a continuing story. After each episode we stop and look at some of the issues raised, and widen out the discussion. By the end you will know more about all aspects of smoking, and will be able to make up your own mind about it.

WHY DO PEOPLE SMOKE?

TOBACCO ARRIVED IN EUROPE IN THE 16TH CENTURY. MANY EUROPEANS BEGAN TO SMOKE BECAUSE THEY BELIEVED TOBACCO CONTAINED MEDICINE WHICH WOULD BE GOOD FOR THEIR HEALTH.

Today it is well known that the opposite is true, and that smoking can be very dangerous. Yet many people, including young people, continue to smoke.

There are many reasons for this. Some smokers simply enjoy the taste of cigarettes. Or they feel smoking makes them look sophisticated. Some become used to the feel of a cigarette between their fingers, and find the act of taking a drag of a cigarette comforting. Many smokers believe that cigarettes calm their nerves and help them cope with stress. Some even claim cigarettes help them to think more clearly.

The main reason people smoke is that smoking quickly becomes a habit – an addiction. This is because cigarettes and other tobacco products contain a drug called nicotine. Nicotine is a deadly poison. The amount from cigarettes is not enough to kill, but it causes a serious reaction in the body. When tobacco smoke is inhaled, nicotine in the smoke passes through the tiny vessels in the lungs into the bloodstream. The drug reaches the brain in seconds, making the smoker feel relaxed yet alert. Cigarettes also contain other chemicals which harm the body.

Once you have started to smoke, it can be very difficult to stop.

▽ It was December. Kim and Sam Lawrence were shopping for presents with their mother, Barbara.

LET'S GO GET UNCLE PHIL HIS PIPE.

I WISH WE COULD BUY HIM SOMETHING ELSE. I HATE THE SMELL OF HIS TOBACCO.

▽ Whilst Mrs Lawrence paid for the pipe they had chosen, Sam and Kim explored the shop.

WHAT'S THAT?

THAT'S SNUFF. IT'S TOBACCO POWDER THAT YOU SNIFF THROUGH YOUR NOSE. GRANDAD LAWRENCE USED TO USE IT.

COME ON, MUM. WE'VE GOT TO GET AUNTIE ANGIE'S PRESENT BEFORE THE SHOP CLOSES.

Mrs Lawrence had told Kim that she started smoking when she was a teenager, because her friends were doing it. ▽

I'LL JUST FINISH MY CIGARETTE.

△ The shop didn't allow smoking, so Sam and Kim went on ahead.

MAYBE WE SHOULD GET MUM THIS BOOK ON STOPPING SMOKING FOR CHRISTMAS.

I THINK SHE'D NEED MORE HELP THAN THAT. SHE'S BEEN SMOKING FOR YEARS.

◁ Kim told her mum about the Stop Smoking book.

IT'S NOT SO EASY TO STOP. THE REAL TRICK IS NOT TO START IN THE FIRST PLACE.

DON'T WORRY. YOU'LL NEVER CATCH ME SMOKING.

Do you think Kim's mum is right?

Cigarettes are by far the most popular tobacco product, and the most widely available. But as Kim and Sam have seen, tobacco is also available in other forms.

Cigars and pipe-tobacco are lighted and inhaled through the mouth, like cigarettes. Snuff is powdered tobacco which is either sniffed or placed between the lip and gum. It was popular in Europe in the 18th century, but is not used much today. Chewing tobacco is also sold. All of these products contain nicotine.

Kim knows that her mum would find giving up cigarettes very difficult, because she has been smoking a long time.

Mrs Lawrence is addicted to nicotine. Her body has become so used to the drug that she would find it hard to do without it. Very often, smoking becomes a ritual. Some people smoke as many as 60 cigarettes a day. Often they may not even realise that

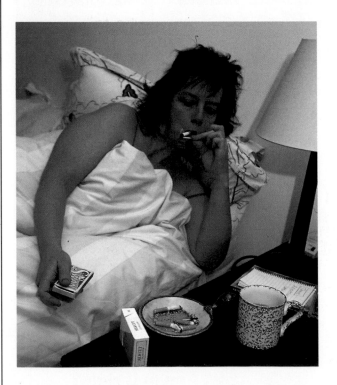

they have lit another cigarette. It has become an automatic reaction. With some smokers the habit is severe. "Chain smokers" smoke one cigarette after another. They may even light up a second cigarette without realising that they haven't finished smoking the first.

Like Barbara Lawrence, many parents do not want their children to smoke.

Most adults are fully aware of the dangers involved in smoking, even if they cannot give up themselves or feel they do not want to. As Mrs Lawrence knows, the only certain way not to let smoking become a problem is not to start in the first place.

STARTING TO SMOKE

TWO-THIRDS OF ALL ADULTS DO NOT SMOKE. MOST OF THOSE THAT DO SMOKE START WHEN THEY ARE YOUNG, USUALLY IN THEIR EARLY TEENS.

Research suggests that if you have not started by the time you are 20, it is likely that you will not become a smoker.
People start to smoke for different reasons. Older smokers may say they started because when they were younger, most of the people they knew smoked. In the past, people were less aware of the dangers involved, and there were no restrictions on advertising. Some adverts even made cigarettes appear to be good for you!

Some young people start to smoke because they say it makes them feel grown up. Some try cigarettes because they want to look big and impress others. Or they could be copying someone they admire. If your friends smoke, there is often a lot of pressure on you to take up smoking too. It can be hard to refuse when those around you are doing it. Whatever their reason for starting, people who take up smoking have not always considered the possible consequences later on.

Some people begin to smoke simply because they have been told they mustn't. It is their way of rebelling, of showing they are different.

▽ Marcus, a boy at Kim's school, had invited her to go to the cinema with his friends. Kim was really excited.

I NEED TO STOP AT THE SHOP FOR A MINUTE.

I'LL COME IN WITH YOU.

I DIDN'T KNOW YOU SMOKED.

OF COURSE I DO. IT'S REALLY GREAT.

△ Kim was shocked to find Marcus buying cigarettes.

YOU'RE NOT SIXTEEN YET. THAT SHOPKEEPER SHOULDN'T HAVE SOLD THEM TO YOU.

IF YOU CAN PAY, MOST SHOPS ROUND HERE DON'T CARE WHO THEY SELL THEM TO.

▷ Kim was annoyed that some shopkeepers were prepared to break the law.

NO I DON'T WANT ONE.

GO ON—YOU'LL LIKE IT I PROMISE.

YOU'RE NOT SCARED ARE YOU?

▷ After the film, Marcus lit another cigarette and offered one to Kim.

△ To impress Marcus, Kim decided to try a cigarette.

"IT'S HORRIBLE!"

▽ Kim felt dizzy and slightly sick.

"IT'S ALWAYS A BIT STRANGE AT FIRST. YOU'LL SOON GET USED TO IT."

Christmas Day...

◁ Marcus was right. By Christmas Kim had grown to like cigarettes, and had begun to steal her mum's.

"YOU SAID YOU'D NEVER SMOKE. IT'S BAD FOR YOU."

"YOU'RE JUST A KID – YOU DON'T UNDERSTAND."

▷ Sam noticed Kim sneak out of the house, and followed her.

"MUM WOULDN'T LIKE YOU SMOKING."

▷ Kim told Sam that her friends smoked, and it made her feel grown-up.

"I CAN GIVE UP ANY TIME I WANT TO. AND YOU'D BETTER NOT TELL ANYONE ABOUT THIS."

The reaction to the first cigarette varies from person to person.

Some people find it makes their head spin and gives them a slightly dizzy feeling. Others feel sick. Nicotine causes all these effects, which are in fact symptoms of very mild poisoning. It seems odd that people who dislike their first cigarette carry on smoking. Kim did not enjoy her first cigarette very much, but Marcus and his friends persuaded her to keep trying. As Marcus had predicted, she quickly became used to the taste – and to the feeling she got from smoking. Addiction can happen very quickly.

There are strict laws about the age at which you can buy cigarettes.

Despite this, cigarettes are often available, even to very young people. As Kim found out, many shops are prepared to break the law. Young people who are determined to smoke will find ways to get hold of cigarettes. If a shop refuses to serve them, they may ask someone who looks older to buy them on their behalf. Or they may steal them from someone else's packet, as Kim has done.

Surveys carried out in Britain have shown that young people often take up smoking at the age of 11 or 12, at the time when they are changing schools.

This can be a particularly difficult time for many people. If you are trying to make new friends, it can be hard to refuse to do what they are doing – even if you know it is wrong. You want to be accepted. But remember that real friends will not try to force you to do things you don't want to do.

WHAT EFFECTS DOES SMOKING HAVE ON YOUR HEALTH?

TO MAKE CIGARETTES, TOBACCO LEAVES ARE DRIED AND SHREDDED, THEN ROLLED INTO TUBES. THE SMOKE FROM BURNING TOBACCO CONTAINS MORE THAN 4,000 GASES AND CHEMICALS, MANY OF WHICH ARE POISONOUS.

These substances include ammonia, found in cleaning fluids, carbon monoxide, the deadly gas in car exhaust fumes, and tar. When cigarette smoke is inhaled, these substances pass into the body.
A smoker breathes cigarette smoke directly through the mouth into the bronchial tubes which lead to the lungs. Tiny particles stick to the walls of the tubes, causing irritation. The cigarette smoke which passes into the lungs leaves behind a sticky brown tar. This tar contains chemicals known to cause cancer. Nine out of ten deaths from lung cancer are caused by smoking.

Smoking can also lead to cancer of the mouth and throat. It can cause other breathing problems. The body produces mucus to try to protect itself from the effects of tar. This can sometimes clog the air passages and the lungs, so they can no longer work properly. This disease, emphysema, can be fatal.

Smokers also run the risk of developing heart disease. Because of the effects of nicotine and carbon monoxide on the blood, the heart has to work harder to get the oxygen it needs. This can lead to a heart attack. Nearly a quarter of all deaths from heart disease are caused by smoking.

Smoking can damage the mouth (1), throat (2), bronchial tubes (3), lungs (4) and heart (5).

◁ Sam's term project was about smoking and pollution.

FILTERS DON'T STOP ALL THE TAR GETTING THROUGH. TAR FROM CIGARETTES CLOGS UP SMOKERS' LUNGS.

I DON'T WANT TO DO THE QUESTIONAIRE ABOUT WHY PEOPLE SMOKE. IT'LL UPSET MY FAMILY.

▷ After school, Sam and his friends Habib and Andrew discussed their project homework.

MY UNCLE HAS LUNG CANCER. HE KNEW SOMETHING WAS WRONG FOR AGES, BUT STILL KEPT ON SMOKING.

I DON'T KNOW HOW PEOPLE CAN GO ON SMOKING WHEN THEY KNOW IT'S SO BAD FOR THEM.

NEITHER DO I.

MY SISTER SMOKED ALL THE TIME SHE WAS EXPECTING HER BABY. MUM REALLY WORRIED ABOUT IT.

▷ Sam and his friends were beginning to understand the real dangers of smoking.

Why was Andrew's mum worried about his sister smoking?

Andrew is aware that his sister took a very big risk by smoking when she was pregnant.
When a woman is expecting a baby, any substance which enters her bloodstream also enters the bloodstream of her unborn child. So the nicotine she takes in through smoking can affect the child. Research has shown that pregnant women who smoke stand a higher risk of their baby dying than those who don't. There is also a greater chance that babies will be born prematurely, or will not weigh as much as they should.

Like many smokers, Habib's uncle thought that smoking would not do him any harm.
Often, smokers are tempted to think "it won't happen to me". They might tell you about people who have smoked all their lives and lived to a very old age. For some people this is certainly the case, but it does not mean that smoking has not affected their health. The medical evidence suggests that smokers are putting their lives at risk. People die every day from diseases which have been directly caused by their smoking.

Sam's teacher has helped the class to understand that the long-term effects of smoking are devastating.
Sometimes smokers themselves are not aware that the diseases caused by smoking usually occur gradually, after someone has been smoking for many years. Because they feel fine at the present time, smokers may be ignoring the fact that they are running a large risk of serious illness at some point later in life.

WHAT OTHER PROBLEMS DOES SMOKING CAUSE?

THE RISK OF MAJOR ILLNESS CAUSED BY SMOKING IS WELL KNOWN. ONE ESTIMATE SUGGESTS THAT THE TOBACCO INDUSTRY NEEDS 300 NEW SMOKERS EVERY DAY, JUST TO REPLACE THOSE WHO HAVE DIED.

However, apart from the health hazards, smoking can also lead to less obvious problems.

Smokers may find that they enjoy food less because cigarettes can affect the way that food tastes. Tar and nicotine deposits can build up on the teeth, making them discoloured. A smoker's fingers may be stained yellow from holding cigarettes. A great many smokers complain of a "smoker's cough". This is the body's way of trying to get rid of some of the tar that has settled in the bronchial tubes, by producing extra mucus to clear the lungs. It is usually worst in the mornings, when the smoker has just woken up.

Smoking also makes people less fit. Many smokers get out of breath very easily, and take longer to recover from any form of exercise than non-smokers. These symptoms can signal the beginnings of serious health problems. Often, however, smokers choose to ignore the symptoms, or do not realise how great the risks are.

Your ability to play and enjoy sport could be damaged by smoking.

▽ As part of the project Sam's class had to design posters about smoking.

▷ Sam told Kim that he had learned in class that smoking now can cause serious illnesses later on.

▽ Kim refused to listen. She tore up Sam's poster and stormed out.

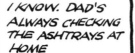

▽ Sam was pleased with his poster and asked to take it home.

▽ Nobody seemed very happy that evening. Kim and Sam weren't talking to each other, and their dad, Joe, was also annoyed.

▽ Phil apologised for being late.

HAVE A GOOD TIME. I'M GLAD YOU'RE NOT TAKING THE CAR. YOU'RE BOUND TO HAVE A FEW DRINKS.

THAT'S OUR BUS. WE'LL HAVE TO RUN TO CATCH IT!

▽ Phil wasn't able to run quickly, and they missed the bus.

I'LL BE ALRIGHT IN A MINUTE.

YOU USED TO BE SUCH AN ATHLETE. YOU COULD BEAT ME ANY DAY.

I'M JUST OUT OF SHAPE, THAT'S ALL. I NEED TO EXERCISE.

◁ Joe was surprised at how long it took Phil to get his breath back.

MAYBE IT WOULDN'T BE A BAD IDEA TO CUT DOWN ON THE SMOKING, TOO.

Why do you think Phil is out of breath?

Cigarettes and all other tobacco products now carry a warning about the health hazards involved in smoking. However, the message is obviously not getting through as well as it should.

Phil used to be an athlete, but now finds it difficult to run even a short distance. This is because his lungs have been damaged by smoking over a long period. Yet he is choosing to ignore this signal. Sometimes this kind of warning is just not enough to alter the way people behave.

As Andrew and Sam know, the other great risk from smoking is fire.

A great many fires are caused by cigarettes or matches not being put out properly. Many people have been killed because they have fallen asleep in bed with a lighted cigarette, and set fire to bedclothes. Certain places have banned smoking completely because of the risk of fire. These include factories, where people work with chemicals and materials which burn easily, and public buildings which sometimes hold large crowds.

In some parts of the world, huge areas of land have been destroyed by forest fires.

Often these fires have been started by just one cigarette or match thrown away carelessly, perhaps from a passing car. Because the land is dry, small fires can quickly take hold and get out of control. Trees, plants and animals die. Many people have also been killed trying to escape these fires.

PASSIVE SMOKING

RESEARCH HAS PROVED THAT SMOKERS ARE NOT ONLY PUTTING THEIR OWN HEALTH AT RISK BY SMOKING.

"Passive smoking" – breathing in the smoke coming from other people's cigarettes – greatly increases our chances of developing serious health problems, even if we are not smokers ourselves. If you have ever walked into a room where lots of people are smoking, you will have noticed smoke filling the air. Smoke can get into people's hair and clothes, and make them smell unpleasant. Passive smoking can make you cough, or give you a sore throat, a runny nose or headache. It can be particularly harmful to people who suffer from asthma. Scientists have now shown that passive smokers also run the risk of developing the same kinds of major diseases as regular smokers. For this reason more and more people are calling for a ban on smoking in all public places.

Cigarette smoke can make your eyes sting, or make you feel slightly sick.

△ It was April 21st – Marcus's birthday. He had invited Kim to join in the family party.

▽ After he had finished his meal, Marcus's father lit up a cigarette.

EXCUSE ME. WOULD YOU MIND PUTTING YOUR CIGARETTE OUT.

YES, I WOULD MIND, AS A MATTER OF FACT.

I'M SORRY, BUT IF I'D WANTED TO BREATHE IN YOUR SMOKE, I WOULDN'T HAVE SAT IN THE **NO SMOKING** SECTION.

I CAN REMEMBER A TIME WHEN YOU COULD SMOKE WHEN AND WHERE YOU WANTED TO. NOBODY BOTHERED YOU.

ACTUALLY SMOKING'S OKAY, BUT I STILL DON'T LIKE PEOPLE SMOKING WHEN I'M EATING.

△ Realising he was in the wrong, Marcus's father put out his cigarette.

Should restaurants ban smoking altogether?

People's views about smoking have changed a great deal over the years. Marcus's father remembers a time when nobody minded if you smoked. Smoking was seen to be fashionable. Advertising companies encouraged people, particularly women, to take up smoking. They always showed smokers having a good time, and tried to give the impression that smoking made people attractive. One cigarette company even used doctors to advertise its cigarettes.

Nowadays there are many places in which smoking is not allowed. Most shops, cinemas, libraries, buses and other forms of transport have banned smoking altogether.

Restaurants usually have smoking and no-smoking areas. These are designed to give people a choice of whether they wish to be in a smoky atmosphere or not. However, although the restaurant can say where smokers should sit, it has no control over the smoke from their cigarettes. In smaller places, the smoke from one area can easily drift into the other, and this can be annoying.

Many people have strong opinions about smoking. It has been said that smokers have the right to choose to smoke, even knowing the damage they may do to themselves. However, anti-smoking organisations call for a complete ban on smoking in public places. They say that smokers should not have the right to put other people's health at risk through passive smoking.

THE SMOKING INDUSTRY

SMOKING IS BIG BUSINESS. EVERY YEAR TOBACCO COMPANIES EARN BILLIONS OF POUNDS FROM THE SALE OF THEIR PRODUCTS. THEY SPEND MILLIONS ON ADVERTISING, TO ENCOURAGE MORE PEOPLE TO BUY.

Tobacco is grown in most parts of the world. Tobacco companies pay farmers to grow the crop. In many cases, the farmers can make more money growing tobacco than growing food.

In some developing countries this has had serious consequences. Much-needed food crops are not planted, because the land is being used to grow tobacco. Tobacco farmers also use a lot of pesticides to make sure the harvest is large. Pesticides can get into drinking water, drift onto food crops and harm animals.

In recent years the hazards of smoking have become clear. Governments have forced cigarette companies to print a health warning on every packet. Tobacco companies started to produce different "strengths" of cigarettes, containing high, middle or low amounts of tar. Sales of high tar brands have fallen in countries where people are aware of the dangers. Yet these brands are still popular in the developing world where health education is not as effective.

Tobacco uses up the goodness from the soil, making it less fertile for other crops.

I THOUGHT CIGARETTE ADVERTISING WAS BANNED ON TV.

◁ Sam was watching sport on TV with his dad. He was surprised to see cigarette brands advertised on racing cars.

ONLY DIRECT ADVERTISING. TOBACCO COMPANIES SPONSOR THESE EVENTS. THEY CAN REACH A LOT OF PEOPLE THIS WAY.

THEY WON'T BAN ADVERTISING OR SMOKING ITSELF ALTOGETHER. PEOPLE MAKE TOO MUCH MONEY FROM IT.

MY TEACHER SAID IT COSTS A LOT OF MONEY JUST TO LOOK AFTER PEOPLE WHO ARE ILL BECAUSE THEY SMOKE.

I THINK ALL ADVERTS SHOULD BE BANNED. IT MAKES SMOKING GLAMOROUS. THAT'S WHY KIM STARTED.

WHOOPS! I SHOULDN'T HAVE SAID THAT.

△ Sam realised what he had said.

I WISH I'D NEVER STARTED. IT'S A TERRIBLE HABIT TO GET INTO. I'D LIKE TO STOP.

▷ Joe told Barbara what Sam had said. They decided to confront Kim.

OK, SO I'VE BEEN SMOKING! YOU'D THINK I'D KILLED SOMEONE.

YOU COULD WELL BE KILLING YOURSELF.

LET'S MAKE A DEAL, THEN. I'LL STOP SMOKING IF YOU WILL.

△ When things had cooled down Barbara talked to Kim again.

Should all cigarette adverts be banned?

As Joe Lawrence said, nowadays the governments of many countries have banned direct advertising of cigarettes on television.

To get around this, some tobacco companies sponsor sports events. This means that when TV programmes show these events, the name of the company will be shown or mentioned. It also suggests a link between smoking and sport, which is considered to be healthy.

Governments in Western countries no longer allow cigarette adverts to link smoking with success and health.

To overcome this, posters advertising cigarettes have become more and more unusual. Often the cigarette brand is not even mentioned. Companies have found ways of suggesting a brand just by using a particular colour. Others use striking images to bring to mind the name of their product.

All over the world, governments make a lot of money from taxes on cigarettes.

In Britain three-quarters of the price of a packet of cigarettes is tax, which goes to the government. The amounts involved are so great, that governments have come to rely on the money they receive. Yet governments could save a great deal on health care. It costs millions every year to look after people who are ill from smoking-related diseases.

13mg TAR 0·9mg NICOTINE
SMOKING WHEN PREGNANT HARMS YOUR BABY
Health Departments' Chief Medical Officers

MAIDEN

STOPPING SMOKING

MANY SMOKERS WOULD LIKE TO STOP. BUT THE HABIT OF SMOKING CAN BE HARD TO BREAK. IT DOES NOT HELP TO BLAME SMOKERS FOR BEING ADDICTED.

Most people agree that to be successful a person must really want to stop. Smokers must make the decision for themselves.

Smokers often have mistaken ideas about what will happen if they stop. Some assume they'll get fat. If they replace cigarettes with snacks, they will put on weight. But stopping smoking itself does not make you fat. Some people gradually cut down the number of cigarettes they smoke. Others stop smoking altogether straight away. Hypnosis and acupuncture are sometimes used to take away the urge to smoke. Special products can help smokers give up. Nicotine chewing gum, and patches which are attached to the skin like a plaster, help reduce the craving for cigarettes, by giving a temporary boost of nicotine.

Taking the decision to stop can be as hard as stopping itself.

YOU KNOW I'VE GIVEN UP. SO HAS MUM.

EVERYONE'S OUT—THEY'LL NEVER KNOW. COME ON, HAVE ONE. IT WON'T DO YOU ANY HARM.

▷ It was now a month since Kim and Barbara had stopped smoking.

IT *DOES* DO YOU HARM. FOR ONE THING, IT MAKES YOUR BREATH SMELL—NOT TO MENTION WHAT IT DOES TO YOUR INSIDES.

▽ Later, Kim talked to her mum.

MARCUS THINKS GIVING UP SMOKING IS A JOKE. HE'S NO IDEA HOW HARD IT IS.

I KNOW IT'S DIFFICULT, EVEN WITH THE NICOTINE PATCHES. YOUR DAD'S GETTING FED UP WITH MY MOODS.

△ Kim was annoyed with Marcus for trying to persuade her to smoke again.

▽ A week later, Barbara was having lunch with Phil's wife, Angie.

MAYBE I WILL JUST HAVE ONE. IT MIGHT CALM MY NERVES.

IT'S AT TIMES LIKE THIS I REALLY MISS CIGARETTES. WHEN EVERYONE ELSE IS SMOKING.

WELL HELP YOURSELF TO ONE OF MINE IF YOU REALLY WANT ONE.

Did Angie help by offering Barbara a cigarette?

Kim now feels that smoking is not an attractive habit.

The smell of cigarette smoke lingers in people's clothes and in their hair. Smokers may also find that cigarettes make their breath smell. Non-smokers are often put off by these things.

Stopping smoking deprives the body of the nicotine it is used to.

People may become moody and irritable as their bodies slowly try to adjust to this change. They may feel a lot of stress and be easily upset. Barbara is worried that Joe is fed up with her moods. But the moods are the fault of the nicotine, not the person.

Many smokers find the hardest part of giving up is being in social situations.

Often when people around them are smoking, the desire to smoke can be very strong indeed. Those who are smoking can help by not offering cigarettes to people they know are trying to stop.

Like Barbara, some former smokers do go back to smoking.

They may explain this by saying they were under great stress, lacked willpower or were feeling fed-up or unhappy. Some start again to cope with a difficult situation, and continue after the situation has passed. Many find they are so used to smoking that they miss the physical act of unwrapping the packet, or the feel of a cigarette between their fingers. Others miss a cigarette after a meal, and find it hard not to light up then. Smoking becomes such a part of people's lives that they need help from friends and family in order to stop successfully.

WHAT CAN BE DONE ABOUT SMOKING?

A SURVEY FOUND THAT A QUARTER OF THOSE ASKED HAD TRIED THEIR FIRST CIGARETTE BEFORE THEY WERE TEN. FOR THE TOBACCO INDUSTRY, EVERY YOUNG PERSON ADDICTED TO SMOKING MEANS YEARS OF PROFIT.

A full understanding of the facts about smoking might help us to decide it's best never to start.
If the health hazards involved in smoking are so bad, why don't governments ban smoking altogether? The truth is that governments make a great deal of money from taxing cigarettes. A government that banned smoking completely would face pressure from the tobacco industry, and would be accused of taking away people's right to choose. It would lose the votes of many smokers, and would be unlikely to be re-elected.

It has been suggested that cigarettes should be made even more expensive. But putting up the price of a product which is addictive may not discourage people from buying it. Certainly there should be tougher action taken against shopkeepers who sell cigarettes to young people. Some organisations call for a ban on all forms of advertising, and for even more places to be made into no-smoking areas.

Perhaps everyone should be given information about the problems and dangers of smoking at an early age.

▽ Barbara began to smoke regularly again. But the family persuaded her to have another try at stopping.

I'M REALLY DETERMINED THIS TIME. I JUST HOPE YOU AND THE KIDS CAN PUT UP WITH MY MOODS.

DON'T WORRY. WE'RE ALL BEHIND YOU.

▽ Kim had heard her mum and dad talking.

I THINK YOU SHOULD PUT THE MONEY YOU SAVE NOT SMOKING INTO A SPECIAL BANK ACCOUNT.

GOOD IDEA. CIGS ARE SO EXPENSIVE, YOU'D SOON HAVE A SMALL FORTUNE TO SPEND ON YOURSELF.

▽ Later Kim ran into Marcus.

I'M THINKING OF STOPPING MYSELF. PEOPLE HAVE TOLD ME I SMELL LIKE AN ASHTRAY.

I'M SORRY I GAVE YOU A HARD TIME ABOUT NOT SMOKING.

I TRIED TO BLAME YOU, BUT IT WAS MY DECISION TO START IN THE FIRST PLACE.

▽ Kim was glad to be with Marcus again.

I'LL HELP YOU TO STOP. IF I CAN DO IT, YOU CAN.

Kim's idea of putting money away has helped many smokers to stop.

Cigarettes are expensive, so the money saved through not smoking can build up quickly. People see their savings grow each week and know that this is money which would otherwise almost literally have been burned. In rewarding themselves from time to time by buying something special, they are strengthening their decision not to smoke any more. They start to look forward to the next "reward".

Barbara, Kim and Marcus are going to have to work hard not to smoke again in the future.

Barbara is determined not to start smoking again. No Smoking Days have helped some addicted smokers like her to take the decision to give up. Kim is annoyed that she started to smoke at all. She understands that she had the right to refuse the cigarette Marcus offered her. She chose to accept because she wanted to impress him. Marcus now feels he was wrong to persuade her to start. Nobody should put pressure on someone else to take up smoking.

People who are trying to give up need a lot of support from those around them.

Some smokers have found that giving up at the same time as others who want to stop can help. Anyone who is having difficulty can discuss the problem with people who are in the same situation, who understand how they are feeling.

WHAT CAN WE DO?

HAVING READ THIS BOOK, YOU WILL UNDERSTAND MORE ABOUT WHY PEOPLE SMOKE, AND THE EFFECT SMOKING CAN HAVE ON OUR LIVES.

If you have thought about taking up smoking, or have tried it already, you need to consider the danger it can be to your health. Remember smoking is not glamorous. You only have to look at an ashtray full of cigarette ends to see that. If you do smoke, don't offer cigarettes to your friends. By encouraging others to smoke, you are putting them at risk too. You can reduce the amount of tar and nicotine you take into your body by taking fewer puffs or smoking less of each cigarette. This still does not make cigarettes safe, though. Some smokers find giving up tobacco difficult; others don't. As soon as you give up, the health risks begin to decrease.

ASH (Action on Smoking and Health)
102 Clifton Street
London EC2A 4HW
Tel: 0207 739 5902
E-mail:
action.smoking.health@dial.
 pipex.com
Website:
www.ash.org.uk

QUIT
102 Gloucester Place
London W1H 3DA
Tel: 0207 487 2858
Smokers' Quitline:
0207 487 3000

SMOKING AFFECTS EVERYONE – NOT JUST THE PEOPLE WHO ARE SMOKING.

Adults can help by understanding that young people are often copying them when they smoke.

The children of smokers are more likely to take up the habit too. Anyone who is trying to stop smoking may be able to get support or advice from some of the organisations listed on these pages. Make sure other people know if you are trying to give up, and if possible, give up with friends so that you can help support each other.

If you know someone who has stopped, help them by giving praise and encouragement. It can be difficult – but it can be done.

Health and Safety Executive
See local telephone directory for details

Tacade
The Advisory Council on Alcohol and Drug Education
The Crescent
1 Hulme Place
Salford, M5 4QA
Tel: 0161 745 8925
E-mail:
ho@tacade.demon.co.uk
Website:
www.tacade.com

Cancer Research Campaign
6-10 Cambridge Terrace
London
NW1 4JL
Tel: 0207 224 1333
Website:
www.CRC.org.uk

British Heart Foundation
14 Fitzhardinge Street
London
W1H 4DH
Tel: 0207 935 0185
Website:
www.bhf.org.uk

Ulster Cancer Foundation
40 Eglantine Avenue
Belfast
BT9 6DX
Tel: 0232 663281

Department of Health, Australia
GPO Box 9848
Canberra
ACT 2601 Australia
Tel: 010 616 289155

INDEX

addiction 4, 6, 10
advertising 7, 20, 21, 23, 27
asthma 18
attitudes to smoking 20

bans on smoking 18, 20, 27
breathing problems 11, 18

cancer 11
chain smokers 6
children of smokers 31
cigarette smoke 4, 11
cigars and pipe-tobacco 6

emphysema 11

fire, risk of 17
first cigarette 10, 27
fitness, lack of 14, 17

government action 23, 27

health care costs 23
health hazards and other problems 4,
11, 13, 14, 17, 18, 30
heart disease 11

laws about selling cigarettes 10

nicotine 4, 6, 10, 11, 13, 14, 24, 26,
30

organisations that can help 30-1

passive smoking 18, 20
pregnancy, smoking during 13

reasons for smoking 4, 7
restaurants, smoking in 20

smoker's cough 14
snuff 6
social situations 26
stopping smoking 24, 26, 29, 31

tar 11, 14, 21, 30
tax on cigarettes 23, 27
tobacco industry 14, 21, 23, 27

Photocredits
All the pictures in this book are by Roger Vlitos apart from pages 3, 20 top: Hulton Deutsch;
page 14: Charles de Vere; page 17 bottom: Frank Spooner Pictures.